In one of our American suburbs there lives an attractive young couple who feel as if their lives are totally out of their control.

Less Stress

The 10-Minute Stress Reduction Plan

DAVID & JANET CONGO

Regal Books

A Division of GL Publications
Ventura, California, U.S.A.

Rights for publishing this book in other languages are contracted by Gospel Literature International (GLINT) foundation. GLINT also provides technical help for the adaptation, translation, and publishing of Bible study resources and books in scores of languages worldwide. For further information, contact GLINT, Post Office Box 6688, Ventura, California 93006, U.S.A., or the publisher.

Published by Regal Books
A Division of GL Publications
Ventura, California 93006
Printed in U.S.A.

Library of Congress Cataloging in Publication Data

Congo, David, 1946-
    Less stress.

    Bibliography: p.
    1. Christian life—1960-   . 2. Stress
(Pychology) I. Congo, Janet, 1949-   . II. Title.
BV4501.2.0649   1985   248.4   85-18306
ISBN 0-8307-0968-1

Contents

Contents

The Emblem

The 10-Minute Stress Reduction's emblem—a 10-minute timer—is intended to remind each of us to take 10 minutes in the midst of a stress-filled situation to analyze our resources, to activate our resources and to adjust our plan while affirming our value.

We wish to acknowledge the pioneering work of Dr. Kenneth Blanchard and Dr. Spencer Johnson, co-authors of *The One-Minute Manager.* The format of their book motivated and sparked our creativity and we owe them our debt of thanks.

Introduction

When the alarm rings each morning the Smiths groan, turn over and promptly press the snooze button, hoping for 15 more minutes of sleep. A couple of minutes later, one of the pair suddenly sits bolt upright, looks at the clock and lets out a panicked yell. The other partner rolls out of bed to face another day. Two bleary-eyed children are yanked out of never-never land and commanded to be dressed and with rooms in order in 10 minutes. A short time later this frenzied foursome arrive at the breakfast nook, greeted by boxes of sugar-coated flakes and coffee.

This is just the beginning of the Smiths' daily rat race. John isn't free from his business responsibilities until 10:30 or 11:00 many evenings. Jane is active in business, leads a small-group Bible study, attends PTA meetings, volunteers for many charities and carpools the children to their various activities.

Weekends aren't much better. Between Little League games, soccer games, chores, projects, church responsibilities and entertaining, the perpetual motion never stops. Meanwhile the house is cluttered, the garage should be bulldozed, the garden only produces exotic varieties of weeds and the couple who believe in a consistent date night haven't had one in months. And where are the children in the midst of this craziness? Why, they're in front of the television set.

One recent Sunday afternoon, Jane stared at John's bloodshot, exhausted and frantic eyes. Bursting into tears, she sobbed, "We can't possibly go on living this way. We're in a rat race. We need help!"

What has happened to this young couple? Over the

past 13 years there have been many changes. They've given up exercise; they've become careless about their diet; they've developed an inconsistency in their spiritual life; they've found themselves driven by the expectations of others; they're increasingly dissatisfied with their marital relationship; they've no time for relaxation; their dreams are shattered; living has become a pressure-filled existence; they feel victimized and their life is out of balance. They're not alone, however! The Smiths are experiencing what *Time* magazine calls *burnout*—the disease of modern life.[1]

Up to this point in his experience, when John feels panic he tends to bury his head in the sand and pretend that life's stresses will disappear. In many ways he is like an ostrich who retreats in the midst of a troubling and potentially dangerous situation. He disregards all signs and goes on with life as usual.

This pattern infuriates Jane, who compensates for her feelings of stress, fear and inadequacy by driving herself even more. She becomes the classic workaholic who moves out in many directions, all at one time.

Nobody can totally escape stress, but too much stress can be hazardous to your health. The American Medical Association reports that stress is associated with 75 percent of all modern diseases. Each year approximately one million Americans die from heart disease and high blood pressure and industry spends $50-$70 billion on insurance costs, hospitalization and lost man hours—all because of stress.

Rather than trying to escape from stress, it is more realistic for us to learn how to manage our stress. Let's follow the life of the Smiths who now recognize that they are victims of their frantic life-style and are in desperate need of change. As the story unfolds John and Jane will encounter people who share their strategic principles for taking charge of life. These principles form the basis for The 10-Minute Stress Reduction Plan that can be successfully applied to your own life.

When you have finished reading the book you will have an invaluable tool that can be detached and used during those times of intense pressure. If adjustment is necessary, you will not only be able to see clearly how that adjustment needs to be made but you will be able to carry it out effectively by analyzing and activating your resources. Your stressful situations can be faced with a sense of praise, purpose and planning. Exchanging tiredness for renewed energy, tenseness for relaxation, a troubled spirit for a tranquil one and a sense of torn-ness for a sense of wholeness is all possible by implementing The 10-Minute Stress Reduction Plan in your life.

The Smiths have heard the siren. They are now faced with a choice—balance or burnout?

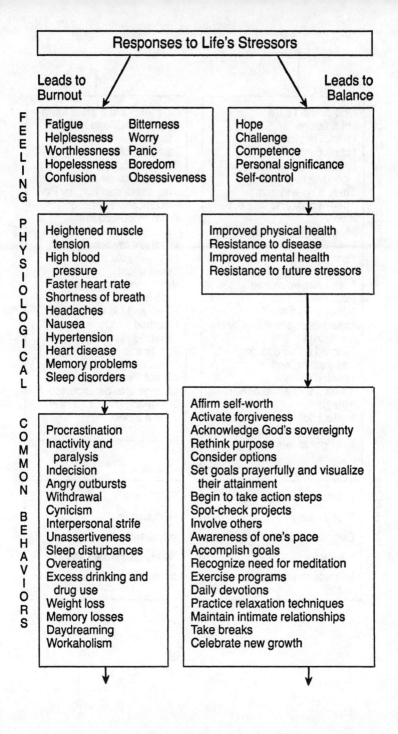

Responses to Life's Stressors

Leads to Burnout

Leads to Balance

FEELING

Fatigue	Bitterness	Hope
Helplessness	Worry	Challenge
Worthlessness	Panic	Competence
Hopelessness	Boredom	Personal significance
Confusion	Obsessiveness	Self-control

PHYSIOLOGICAL

Heightened muscle tension
High blood pressure
Faster heart rate
Shortness of breath
Headaches
Nausea
Hypertension
Heart disease
Memory problems
Sleep disorders

Improved physical health
Resistance to disease
Improved mental health
Resistance to future stressors

COMMON BEHAVIORS

Procrastination
Inactivity and paralysis
Indecision
Angry outbursts
Withdrawal
Cynicism
Interpersonal strife
Unassertiveness
Sleep disturbances
Overeating
Excess drinking and drug use
Weight loss
Memory losses
Daydreaming
Workaholism

Affirm self-worth
Activate forgiveness
Acknowledge God's sovereignty
Rethink purpose
Consider options
Set goals prayerfully and visualize their attainment
Begin to take action steps
Spot-check projects
Involve others
Awareness of one's pace
Accomplish goals
Recognize need for meditation
Exercise programs
Daily devotions
Practice relaxation techniques
Maintain intimate relationships
Take breaks
Celebrate new growth

	THINKING
T H I N K I N G	God doesn't care I'm a failure I think I'm sick I can't think I'm the only one who has gone through this There's no way out There's only one way out If only . . . My past controls me I always fail I can't do anything right God won't forgive me I can't forgive myself Poor me Nobody likes me I need everyone's love and approval I should be able to do everything well I should worry It's easier to avoid difficult things Perfect solutions should be found for everything It is right to feel bad	God and I are a great team This is a challenge to be faced I am capable There is hope I can overcome this This stress can turn my life in a positive direction What resources are available to me? What are my options? I am valuable and competent What can I change in the future? I tried and I learned I learned things that didn't work This is a temporary inconvenience It's not the end Change is to be expected Just trying makes me a winner

	RESULTS
R E S U L T S	Dissatisfaction High anxiety Decreased productivity Insecurity Intimate relationships suffer	Fulfillment Reduced anxiety Increased productivity Newly discovered security Increased intimacy

Step 1
One-Minute Centering

One night, during a dinner party, John and Jane are introduced to Steve and Jenny, a professional couple who are in the midst of a major career shift. Laughter seems to come easily to this exuberant and joyful couple even though rumor has it they are facing the possibility of a move and presently have no steady income to cushion their transition. The Smiths are strangely drawn to this interesting pair and make a date to talk over dinner in a week.

As the week progresses John and Jane experience both apprehension and a mounting curiosity. What makes this couple tick? The week passes frantically and before they know it they are waiting at a restaurant for Steve and Jenny, who arrive walking arm-in-arm and laughing. After expressing how delighted they are to be spending the evening together, the four are escorted to their table by the maitre d'.

John and Jane glance knowingly at one another and John whispers, "Maybe they've had a breakthrough in their career search. They seem to be celebrating. Let's ask!"

After being seated, the question is posed. "You seem so up. Are you celebrating a job change?" A pensive look passes between Steve and Jenny. There's a moment of silence and Steve volunteers, "No. In fact, one of our most promising leads fell through. We got the call just a half hour before leaving home."

Jenny pipes in, "It *really* did and it was terribly disappointing. But we were also looking forward to our evening with you." It is obvious Jenny speaks with sincerity. This is no empty platitude. But how in the world were they able to recover from their disappointment so quickly? After the waiter takes the orders, Jane asks how they coped.

A genuine smile breaks over Jenny's face. "Well, we centered on God."

"What do you mean?"

Steve breaks in, "Awhile back we were at a point in our lives when it seemed like the walls were falling in on us. I was reading about Jacob when he ran away from Esau.

That evening he had a dream. When he woke up he cried out, 'The Lord was here and I didn't even know it.' Jacob's words hit me like a brick. God was there and I didn't even notice."

As John and Jane reflected on what was being said, Jane thought out loud, "I've always believed God is within me. But what does that mean?"

John agrees. "Yeah, I've read that my body is the temple of the living God. But have I ever paid attention to that promise? Now that I think about it, maybe those things that irritate me are *outside* of me. *God* is within me. That must mean He's closer to me than my problems."

"That's fine, John," says Jane, "but how can we acknowledge God's presence when we're stressed out? I know Scripture says not to worry about anything, but isn't that a little unrealistic?"

"I can relate," replies Jenny, "because that was my first response."

"The starting point came for us," Steve continues, "when we deliberately chose to center on God whenever things seemed overwhelming. Even now we sometimes forget that our greatest resource is a pretty big God."

"Yes," Jenny says, "it was at that point we started to make God the heart of our life rather than just tacking Him on when we felt a need to be spiritual."

Without missing a breath Steve adds, "It was Easter when this began happening. We were impressed by Christ's model of centering. Can you imagine being nailed to a cross? In the midst of that agony Jesus focused on God, rather than His pain. He talked as easily with God as with those watching the Crucifixion. Christ's awareness of His Father affected everything else."

"There's nothing outside of my experience with God," Jenny adds, "not my marriage, my parenting, my business, my hobbies—not even my pressures. This sounds

It's not what happens *to* you
that's most important.
It's what happens *within* you.

crazy but when you add food coloring to icing, everything turns the same color. When we make Christ central everything's colored by that choice."

"Let's get practical," sighs John. "How do you do this?"

"Well," says Steve, "whenever we worry we stop to concentrate on God rather than our problem. When we first did this we looked up all the names of God in Scripture. Then we wrote them down on a sheet of paper. Even today we reread this list to remind us of how great God is."

"In fact," Jenny adds, "we read our sheet on the way over here. It's amazing! It never fails to lift our spirits. It's still in my notebook. Would you like to see it?"

John and Jane both express an interest and Steve leaves to get the notebook. Jenny continues talking about another resource sheet containing Scripture promises they find particularly meaningful until Steve's return. In a short time Steve has the notebook and excitedly he and Jenny share their resource sheets with the Smiths (see Worksheets D and E). As they do John and Jane find that their spirits are lifted. They are becoming much more aware of what a phenomenal resource their Lord is.

John asks, "Is this all you do when you center yourselves?"

"No," Steve replies. "We go a step further. We've both chosen one particular verse that's a real stabilizer for us. We added our name to the verse and memorized it."

Jenny adds, "When we begin to feel the stress we stop and concentrate on who God is. Then we praise Him by referring to His many names."

"Next we claim His personal interest in our lives," Steve continues. "We quote our stabilizing verse and pray. What a difference this has made in our lives. It's given us a new perspective."

People who don't give in to

PANIC

in the midst of

STRESS

see GOD as a

P
O
W
PERSONAL
R
F
U
L

RESOURCE!

After such a personal testimony the Smiths feel comfortable enough to share their private thoughts. "When we first met you, it was obvious there was a difference in your outlook. If *we'd* been called a half hour earlier with bad news we would've been depressed. We might've even cancelled out. Focusing on Christ has sure changed your perspective."

"Thanks for the input," Steve replies. "It's exciting when others see growth in us. But this is only the first step in what we call our 10-Minute Stress Reduction Plan."

Steve and Jenny tell the Smiths about a support group they lead and the study on stress and burnout the group has completed. They also tell them about a young couple who would be willing to share more about the Stress Reduction Plan they all use in their lives. John and Jane are interested and Steve promises to call in the morning to set up the meeting.

The Smiths are beginning to see a ray of hope. They seem to be on the trail of something important and for the first time in years feel like they won't have to continue living as the victims of the problems in their lives. Miraculously, it seems to them, an appointment is arranged for breakfast on Wednesday morning.

If you presently face overwhelming stress, turn to Worksheet *A* and proceed with the One-Minute Centering exercise. Then be encouraged by Worksheets *B* and *C*.

Step 2
One-Minute Clarification

Early the following Wednesday John and Jane are facing an alert-looking twosome across the breakfast table. In a few short minutes they learn that Reed has arranged to go into work an hour later in order to give them some of his time. He is a supervisor at a manufacturing plant and his wife Sharon is a homemaker with three children. The Smiths are already fascinated because of the willingness of these strangers to give of themselves.

Because time is precious Reed gets right to the point. "I understand Steve told you about our support group's Stress Reduction Plan."

"Yes," replies John, "and both he and Jenny showed us how to center ourselves."

"Great!" says Reed. "It's all got to start there. Have you tried it?"

Jane replies, "Yes, and we're amazed. Before it always seemed like God was distant and disinterested in our problems."

"We're delighted for you," Sharon interjects. "That one minute of centering will become more meaningful as you practice it. Periodically we set our alarm clock on the hour as a reminder to focus on God."

A little hesitantly John speaks up, "So what's the next step in the plan?"

Reed laughs, "I thought you'd *never* ask. It involves a minute of clarification and boy, is it helpful. You see, I'm responsible for meeting the production deadlines for my area of the plant every two weeks. This means I've got to manage 200 people effectively."

"And I'm responsible," explained Sharon, "at this point in my life for our home and three little human beings, one of whom is still in diapers. Both of our careers are highly stressful and there are times when we feel it!"

"Can we ever relate to that!" respond John and Jane in unison. "There've been many times," John continues, "when we've felt like burned-out light bulbs."

Jane adds, "And there are times when *I* feel like I'm riding an escalator headed into a dark basement. I get

"Tell me what ticks you off
and I will tell you what
makes you tick."

Lloyd John Ogilvie'

depressed and feel helpless, but don't know what to do to stop those feelings."

Reed intervenes, "We've been there, too. But because we're both practical Sharon and I joined the support group studying stress, did a lot of reading, asked many questions and prayed a whole lot. The result is our one minute of clarification."

"We brought along the three parts involved in One-Minute Clarification." Sharon begins by pulling the papers from her purse. "The first thing we did was compile a list of 23 things that cause stress. (See Worksheet *G*.) This tool helps us in the middle of our confusion to identify our primary areas of stress."

Together all four examine the categories causing stress. As they read the list the Smiths point out five areas they believe are causing them stress.

At that point Reed says, "What you really need to do is tackle one stress at a time. Once one is dealt with you can then address another area."

After a minute or two John and Jane agree on their major area of stress. Even seeing the word listed on the stress list causes their anxiety levels to rise, their hearts to beat faster and their muscles to tighten.

Reed senses their stress and before they have a chance to be totally overwhelmed he lays a second piece of paper on the table. Once you've decided what's causing your external stress, then you need to examine the internal stress you place on yourselves."

"One very effective way of doing this," suggests Sharon, "is to examine the shoulds we constantly tell ourselves. We made a list of ours and we'd been persecuting ourselves! Look over our list—you'll be able to relate to a few of these I'm sure." (See worksheet *H*.)

Reed adds, "We all have personal expectations. That's necessary. But too many cause disillusionment and feel-

ings of failure. Choose a *few* expectations you value highly.
Don't be controlled by a multitude of 'shoulds.'"

Once again John and Jane relate to nearly all of the 40
statements. When they read on paper what they have
been telling themselves in their minds, it seems ridiculous.

John asks, "Should we go through this list, choose a
few expectations we will live by and refuse to be driven by
the others?"

"You've got the idea," Sharon replies. "You'll sense
some of your internal stress evaporate."

Because of his time constraint, Reed suggests that the
Smiths spend some time later in the day examining the list
together. He also advises them to write out the expectations they choose for themselves.

"But," Sharon says, "there's a third part to our One-
Minute Clarification. It involves writing down a concise
definition of the particular problem we want to address."

"If we can't define the problem," Reed explains, "we
can't find a solution and we're left with nothing but confusion and pressure. Now at this point if you're *still* having
difficulty defining what the problem is ask yourself, 'What
makes me really angry about this stressful situation?' You
might even list your worries." (See Worksheet *I.*)

Sharon adds, "When you write out your problem you'll
be amazed at your new sense of direction. You'll also
appreciate the emotional release that comes along with it.
Good luck."

Reed looks at his watch and says, "I need to get to the
plant. Let us know how it goes."

After Reed and Sharon leave, John and Jane stay at
their table. They order another cup of tea and begin to
define their problem. At first it seems as if focusing on one
problem is impossible. They are aware of so many. But as
they begin to seriously think about their emotional
responses to stress, they realize that much of their anger

and many of their worries are rooted in one particular area.

After writing down in a concise statement the problem they are planning to confront first, there is an internal sense of relief and Jane verbalizes it first. "I wanted to solve everything at once and I've been getting nowhere. It feels good to know there's one area we can deal with together."

"It does, doesn't it?" agrees John. "I've been ignoring the stresses we've been under—hoping they'd go away. Well, they haven't and we've both gotten more and more miserable. I now feel better about finding solutions."

"In many ways I feel like we're at a turning point in our own relationship," replies Jane.

Her husband agrees. They pay their bill and leave the restaurant with a sense of relief.

If you've centered on God as your primary resource, proceed with the One-Minute Clarification, Worksheet *F*.

Step 3
One-Minute Self-Evaluation

A few days later, Reed phones the Smiths to see if they have focused on one stress-causing problem. Jane tells Reed of their success and asks about the next step in the Stress Reduction Plan.

Reed is pleased with their enthusiasm and asks if she and John will be home on Monday evening of the following week. He also asks if they are willing to have a visitor stop by.

On Monday evening John and Jane open their home to a pastor named Art who is in his late 30s. While dessert is being served they learn that Art is single and has been in the support group with Reed, Sharon, Steve and Jenny. There is such an openness about him that before long they feel as if they've always known him.

Art turns the conversation to the issue at hand when he says, "Well, Reed tells me you've been introduced to the first two phases of our Stress Reduction Plan. Before I tell you about the next principle may I share some of my personal experience as it relates to it?" asks Art.

After receiving two nods of agreement Art proceeds, "I've been the assistant pastor in a growing church for the last eight years. Christmas always makes me nervous. Not only do I face four Christmas Eve services and three more services in the morning, I also have to motivate the choirs, the orchestra and the soloists to attend all of the rehearsals eight weeks prior to the holiday. I've never been satisfied with mediocrity!

"Last year, in the middle of all this pressure, I was criticized by some key people in the church for not being a caring person. You know, many people criticize the character of someone they are frustrated with rather than just expressing disapproval with the person's programs or decisions. Well, I wasn't introducing programs they wanted for their children and even though I can analyze that, it doesn't stop the hurt. During this same time the vacancy for the new senior pastor was filled by a fine man, but someone with a completely different philosophy of ministry.

"Needless to say, I was reeling under the pressure. My ministry had been significant and I had a file full of appreciation notes. But somehow they meant nothing to me after hearing the negative comments. I felt incapable and inadequate. If I wasn't a failure, why was this happening? It seemed like no matter what I did it was never enough. I wondered if a poor spiritual life was the cause of all of this. I also felt totally helpless. I began to feel very sorry for myself and questioned my place in the ministry.

"It was at that low point in my life that I ran into Steve again. It had been years since I'd seen him. Would you believe, I used to date his daughter? Anyway, Steve read my face and asked me what was up. After filling him in on a few of the particulars he suggested we go out to lunch. I was most willing.

"During our lunch Steve said neither of us could deny I had made some mistakes but that didn't prove I was no good. On a napkin, he drew a word equation of the way I'd been choosing to live. I will never forget it—

Mistakes = Personal Failure = I'm no good.

"At that point Steve looked me straight in the eye and asked if I wanted to be any different. Of course I said I wanted to change and he said only God could break up that equation. According to him, I had to get a clear perspective of God's view of me.

"Here I was, a pastor being told by a businessman that I needed a clearer perspective of how God viewed me. It was humbling but he was right.

"Steve went on to say he'd been listening to me talk for over an hour and if he had to summarize my view of myself it would be that I was insignificant, a failure and unappreciated. I'll never forget the caring look that passed over his face as he said firmly, 'Art, all three of those descriptive words are in opposition to what the Lord tells us about ourselves.'

"He then went on to point out that according to Scripture, when God looks at us He sees a highly significant, deeply fallen and greatly loved person. We're highly significant because we're created in the image of God. Just as a book reflects its author, so we reflect God's character. We're deeply fallen because we're all sinners. But God made provision for that in Jesus Christ. When confessed, our sins, mistakes and failures are covered by the blood of Jesus Christ. So when God looks at us He sees us as holy and perfect, clothed in the righteousness of Jesus. Because of Christ's sacrifice our failure is never final."

Art has been so intent on what he's sharing he hasn't noticed tears welling up in John's eyes. Jane is also moved and says, "It feels good to be reminded of how God views us—to realize again that there aren't any risks in our Saviour's love. How different this truth is compared to all the conditions we put on our love."

"Yes," Art replies, "that day Steve took me to Scriptures that showed me again how my Saviour loves me. I hope you don't mind but I brought you both a copy of the list of verses (see Worksheet *K*). No self-evaluation is constructive if it doesn't begin there."

Together the three new friends read through some of the Scripture passages, praising God for His unfathomable love, grace and acceptance.

After refills are made on beverages Art asks if John and Jane know a pastor friend of his named Rev. Creed. "He's seen the Lord miraculously work in his ministry. In fact, his group just experienced a dramatic outpouring of the Lord and he's excited, but emotionally tired out. Lately he's been receiving threats from some jealous individuals. He's scared. Now he retreats from his ministry, spending most of his time alone. He told me he's even asked the Lord to take his life."

The Smiths don't know the pastor but they ask Art

MY VIEW

Mistakes = Personal Failure
Character Flaws

→ I am insignificant, a failure and unappreciated.

GOD'S VIEW

Mistakes ≠ Personal Failure
Character Flaws

→ I am highly significant, deeply fallen and greatly loved.

where his church is located. Art responds quickly, with a twinkle in his eye, "I'm afraid you'll have to forgive me. His name's really Elijah and he can be found in 1 Kings chapter 19.

"A turning point came in my life when I met this prophet through Steve," Art continues. "He pointed out that when dealing with Elijah, the Lord was practical. Elijah really had lost his perspective of God's greatness but the Lord doesn't chastise him for it. Neither does He tell Elijah he has a deep-rooted spiritual problem—as we so often do. Instead He sees that Elijah gets more rest, takes some time off and eats better. Then He helps Elijah re-evaluate his situation and gets him an assistant.

"Because God solves Elijah's problem so practically, I think God affirms his humanness and his ministry. Elijah, on the other hand, is personally renewed, develops more of a team ministry and realizes that God certainly hasn't set him on a shelf. This is an Old Testament example of a New Testament truth. Elijah is now free to return to his ministry."

Without so much as a pause Art continues, "If I can leave Elijah, I'll share how this helped my situation. If I had to define my main problem at the time I met with Steve, it was that the unrealistic demands from the senior pastor, the board members and myself caused great interpersonal strain. And because I felt controlled by others and unable to live up to their expectations, I adopted some unhealthy beliefs.

"I felt I had to be liked by everyone and the way to be liked was to behave the way others expected. I believed I should be able to fulfill these expectations if the Lord had really placed me here and I think I really believed I could do it with no criticism. Underneath it all was the mistaken belief that it was more Christian to please other people than to please myself.

"Thank the Lord for Steve's wise counsel. He forced me to face my misbeliefs and to remember that other people don't determine my value, God does. I achieve out of a sense of adequacy, not ever to determine my adequacy. Then he pointed out that I couldn't possibly please everyone. That is the ultimate impossible dream."

Art pulls a piece of paper out of his Bible and continues, "In my readings I came across a list of healthy beliefs (see Worksheet *L*). I have found this list personally helpful. I often pull it out several times a day and read it aloud."

When he hands it to the Smiths they study it carefully. Jane says, "These are great! When someone asks me to do something I often say yes only because I want other people to like me. Later I feel frustrated with all the things I'm doing for others because I have little time to do what I consider important."

"We've all been there," nods Art. "I've shared with you the first two steps of the One-Minute Self-Evaluation. Do you recall what they are?"

"You bet I do," replies John. "First, we emphasize how God sees us in Scripture. Then we evaluate our belief system and eliminate unhealthy thinking patterns."

"Great," responds Art. "The last step is to conduct a thorough self-evaluation. This is where it's easy to bog down because we aren't sure how to begin. For this reason I've brought a questionnaire that I find helpful (see Worksheet *M*).

"It assists us when evaluating our talents, experiences, strengths and weaknesses. This perspective doesn't allow for arrogance because God is the One at work within us. But we can each stand as tall as is possible."

Art could tell that this was a new thought. They had never undergone a thorough self-evaluation because they

"Jesus died on a cross for me so that I can be free from the misbelief that other people decide my value."

H. Norman Wright[1]

feared being proud and self-centered. Never had they viewed the process as a way to praise their Creator. Somehow the idea now seems possible as they ponder it.

Art continues, "Use this questionnaire to identify the qualities that best describe you. Then decide which of these qualities will help you face and deal with the problem at hand."

John breaks in, "I'm beginning to understand. We need to evaluate the assets God has helped us develop in our lives. These consist of our traits, contacts and even our strengths and weaknesses. Then we select those assets which will help us the most in solving our problem."

"Yes," Jane interrupts with eyes sparkling, "it seems to me that by looking at our assets we're really saying, 'I'm this way therefore I can do this.' Perhaps it could be referred to as the 'I am therefore I can' principle."

Art laughs, "That's exactly how it has worked in my life. I've chosen artistic, perfectionistic, good instructor, motivator and achiever. Then I look back at the problem I've defined in my One-Minute Clarification. In my case, as you remember, the problem was how to deal with everyone else's unrealistic expectations for me."

"So what did you do?" ask the Smiths.

"Well," replies Art, "I knew I was creative so I needed to use this creativity to define the direction I felt the Lord wanted me to move. Then I needed to use my abilities as a teacher to educate my senior pastor and the members of our board why this direction would be beneficial for the church. Lastly, I needed to use my skills as a motivator to persuade others that this was an area where they'd like to help. All this resulted because I acknowledged my strengths and praised God for His work in me."

"That's super," respond John and Jane. "You move in a positive direction because you analyze your resources through God, your situation and yourself."

You have
analyzed
your resources.

Prepare to
activate
those resources.

"That's right," affirms Art. "Now I need to be moving on. I hope the One-Minute Self-Evaluation is helpful. The first time you go through these three steps it'll take you longer than one minute. But after you've prayerfully worked through it all it'll only take you a minute to review it.

"May I challenge you to work through this evaluation before you meet with any more of the people who attend our support group. In fact, you could spend an evening reviewing the resources you now have at your fingertips."

Assuring him that they would set aside some time during the coming weekend to work on this evaluation, the Smiths walk Art to the door. John and Jane are quietly pondering the interest God has shown in their lives. Why, two weeks ago they hadn't even known that Steve, Jenny, Reed, Sharon or Art existed, and now they have five new friends. It's amazing that people who didn't even know them would be willing and able to take time out of their busy schedules to share these new concepts with them. God is so good! With that they straighten up the kitchen, turn off the lights and go to bed.

If you have clarified your problem, proceed with your One-Minute Self-Evaluation, Worksheet *J*.

Step 4
Five-Minute Plan

Early one morning the phone rings and John answers it, discovering to his delight that it's Art. Art asks if they're ready to proceed to the next step in the Stress Reduction Plan. After John assures him that they are ready and willing, Art puts the Smiths in contact with a psychologist and his wife.

John phones and leaves a message with the doctor's answering service. A few moments later their phone rings and Jane finds herself talking to Larry, the psychologist. An appointment is set up for Wednesday evening. They arrange to meet at the church Larry and his wife attend since it is located close to the hospital where Larry's wife works. Once again the Smiths are overwhelmed at the willingness of such busy people to share their time with total strangers.

On Wednesday evening, as they approach the church, they see Art talking with a sharp-looking couple in their early thirties. They park their car, introductions are made, and with that Art leaves for another appointment. The four go inside the church to the appointed room.

Within a short time the Smiths learn that Larry has just completed his doctoral program in psychology. He faces the challenge of developing his own private practice and preparing for the state licensing exam.

It seems to John this would be a highly stressful stage to be in. Yet Larry appears relaxed and eager to reach out. *Perhaps,* John thinks, *Larry or Linda come from a fairly well-to-do family. Maybe they've had a great deal of financial help from their parents.*

His thoughts are interrupted by Linda, who shares that she is still working full time even though they had their first child four months ago. The numerous debts incurred from graduate education make this time away from the baby a necessity for now. Linda has chosen to work the graveyard shift so either she or Larry can be with the baby most of the time.

After being questioned, Linda admits that this is tiring but she says, "It's one of the small steps we've worked out to pay off these debts." She continues, "We've set a deadline of eight months from now for me to stop working full time and move to a part-time position."

It's amazing to the Smiths that there's no self-pity in Linda. She seems to have decided what needs to be done and is doing it. They comment on this and Larry smiles, saying, "What you're saying has everything to do with the next phase of our Stress Reduction Plan."

Linda agrees. "It would be impossible for us to get to this stage if we didn't begin our Stress Reduction Plan by centering ourselves.

"We're facing many stresses in our life—a new baby, financial pressure, a new career and the strain that's put on our marriage relationship. Total panic would incapacitate us, as would self-pity, if we didn't begin by acknowledging that God is our foremost resource. He won't forsake us. He'll work in and through us."

Larry interjects, "I've often found that when I share the concept of centering with some of my clients a few of them are so tense they have to be taught how to relax before they can center on God. Therefore I've made a relaxation tape. They take it and in the comfort of their own home learn to relax the tense muscles in their body."

Looking straight at John and Jane he asks, "If you'd be interested in learning how to do this yourself, I'll give you the tape and summary sheet I give to my clients (see Worksheet O). This is not an addition to the centering process. Rather, it's a way you can relax your body so you'll get the maximum benefit from focusing on your Saviour."

John and Jane acknowledge this fact and read over the summary sheet together. John says, "I've heard so much about relaxation but I must confess I've passed it off as a fad. Maybe I should give it a chance."

Linda speaks up, "I often use this prior to starting the entire Stress Reduction Plan. It makes it easier for me to give God my attention. My centering also seems more focused."

Larry speaks, "Now, recall the problem you've chosen to deal with. Some time has passed since you wrote that down. Do you still see it as the major problem or is it a symptom of a deeper one?"

In response Jane says thoughtfully, "As far as we know it's the main problem. Don't you agree, honey?"

John replies affirmatively and Larry continues, "Fine. The reason we ask you to write the problem down is that by doing so you're able to see the problem more clearly. There's a great ancient oriental proverb. Have you heard it? 'The palest ink is more enduring than the greatest memory.'"

"That's great," responds Jane, "I'm a real list maker. If I don't write things down I'm lost. But there are still so many fires to put out and I really don't know where to begin. Therefore I'm a first class procrastinator. That's why the One Minute Clarification has been so helpful."

John nods his head. "We've talked about this, haven't we, honey? When *I'm* panicked it's almost impossible for me to do the self-evaluation. It's as if I'm frozen and I don't like being that out of control."

Larry smiles and replies, "I appreciate your honesty. We must all *center* on the Lord, *clarify* our problem and *evaluate* our God-given assets.

"Now the next step is to take these resources and put them into a workable plan. We call this step the Five-Minute Plan.

"It's impossible to set up a plan if you haven't clearly defined the problem. That's why the first step of our Five-Minute Plan is to have a specific problem clearly in mind and record it."

"Working harder is not necessarily a solution to one's problems," comments Linda. "I've got a great story. I heard it one night at our support group meeting.

"There was a young man who had admired lumberjacks all his life and had lived around lumbering communities. On his eighteenth birthday he got up enough courage and applied for a job. The boss gladly gave the strong young man a job and by the end of the first day he'd chopped down 10 large trees all by himself. This was an unusual feat and the boss was thrilled.

At the end of the next day he'd cut down eight trees. He was disappointed even though it was still considered respectable. But during the rest of the week, even though he worked just as long and hard, he cut down fewer and fewer trees. By the end of the week the boss called in the humiliated young man.

"'Sir,' he apologized, 'I'm working harder than ever, but I haven't cut down a tree today. Guess I wasn't meant to be a lumberjack.' Then his boss asked him if he'd taken the time to sharpen his ax. The boy replied, 'No sir, I've been too busy working to take the time.' We've got to work sharper and smarter—not necessarily harder."

"That's great," laughs Jane. "Your support group is training both of us!"

"Thanks," responds Linda. "An effective way to work smarter is to brainstorm all the possible solutions to your problem. At this stage, Larry and I often find it helpful to talk this over with someone whose judgment we value."

"Yes," Larry adds, "and as husband and wife you have one another to bounce off possible solutions. But you'll still find it valuable to ask for someone else's input. By the end of this time of brainstorming you'll have a list containing both reasonable and unreasonable options."

Linda smiles and says, "Having a list like this will make you both aware of many more options. You won't feel suf-

"If you think you've exhausted all the options, you haven't."

Robert Schuller

focated or locked into one option."

John nods his head and adds, "Well, I know I make better decisions if I have several options rather than only one or two. Maybe that's why I've been so bogged down with the problem we're facing. I really thought there was only one option and I didn't like it."

Larry nods his head in agreement. "That makes me think of something I read the other day, 'If you think you've exhausted all the possibilities, you probably haven't.' That's why discussing your problem with a wise third party can be so valuable.

"Let's review. The first step in the Five-Minute Plan is to write down a concise summary of the problem. Then you both need to brainstorm as many solutions to the problem as you can. Next you choose the best solution and record it at the top of a clean sheet of paper."

Linda laughs, "Now the fun begins because from this point on you'll be making positive steps in solving your problem. You'll feel like victors rather than victims."

Both John and Jane are ready for those feelings. They're also experiencing some relief from the stress they've been under for so long.

Larry continues talking, "You'll find it necessary to program your solution into measurable, time-related steps. Personally, we picture our solution at the top of a flight of stairs. Each step, then, is something we choose to do which moves us closer to our goal."

Linda smiles, "When we were first introduced to the Five-Minute Plan we decided to work on our marriage relationship because it had taken a lower priority than we desired during the pressures of Larry's doctoral program. We decided to schedule a weekend away for fun, prayer and planning. Let me sketch a picture of the way we broke that decision down."

For the next few moments Linda sketches. Then she

hands the sketch over to John. "This is such a simple illustration and yet we'd gotten so far away from our priorities this is where we had to begin. It felt great to be doing something. The reason we think it's necessary to write goals down is because they're nothing more than unfulfilled wishes if we don't. That's frustrating."

The Smiths nod their heads in agreement and look closely at the sketch.

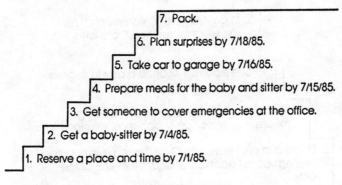

Solution: Weekend away for fun and planning.
Date: 7/20/85

7. Pack.

6. Plan surprises by 7/18/85.

5. Take car to garage by 7/16/85.

4. Prepare meals for the baby and sitter by 7/15/85.

3. Get someone to cover emergencies at the office.

2. Get a baby-sitter by 7/4/85.

1. Reserve a place and time by 7/1/85.

Problem: Marriage has become low priority

When John and Jane finish reading the paper, Larry begins to speak. "We had a wonderful weekend together. During those three days we created another chart. This

Goal: To love each other more.

10. Each be responsible for planning one surprise each week.

9. Plan a weekend away every three months.

8. Meet on Sunday evenings to affirm each other for the progress we're making and adjust where needed.

7. Physically demonstrate our affection in front of the baby.

6. In conflict, use "I" statements (I feel this way) rather than those attacking "you" statements.

5. Phone each other once a day to express love.

4. Pray together once a day, not including meals. Pray specifically about our relationship.

3. Share a cup of tea daily. Over the tea express only feelings about each other and the events of the day.

2. Greet each other at the door daily.

1. Have a date night each week. Alternate the planning. Time: Monday evening.

one was designed to help us to increase our love for each other. I realize this might be offensive to some people, but you've got to realize that we were desperate for a change in our relationship. We wanted a healthy marriage daily. I brought along this chart. Do you want to see it?"

Both John and Jane begin to see that their dreams can become a reality, one step at a time.

"Wow," exclaims John, "you really want to see change, don't you?"

"You bet," replies Linda. "We aren't ready to be another divorce statistic."

"You see, it seems to me," Larry continues, "life is a do-it-to-yourself project. It's true—we can't afford to avoid our problems. We must clearly define them, propose varied solutions, pinpoint the best one and then break it down into small steps."

With that Linda breaks in, "But don't stop there. It's time to let your fantasy run wild. Imagine what it's going to feel like when you reach your goal. Enjoy the thought. In fact, we recommend you write your goal, as if it is completed, on a 3x5-inch card. Read the card daily. My card says, 'I love Larry more than ever before. I'm a more loving person.' I also thank the Lord daily that He's creating me into a more loving person."

Larry smiles and says, "I have my card too. I pull it out whenever I'm caught in traffic or find myself waiting for someone. I'd rather focus on the goal rather than the problem. And don't be afraid to daydream in vivid detail. Imagine how you're going to feel when your problem is solved. Imagine the difference it'll make in your life-style.

"In my case I imagine what it'll be like to see Linda enthusiastic about me and our being together. I even imagine some of the conversations we might have, some of our dates and the difference it's going to make behind closed doors."

Linda laughs, "You know, it's fun to make a difference in your life! And I apologize, but I've got to go. My shift begins in half an hour. I've surely enjoyed our time together."

The Smiths express their gratitude to Larry and Linda. Larry then suggests they pray. Taking their hands he begins:

> Lord, thank you that even though you are the Eternal God and Creator of this vast universe you are most concerned about the minutest details of our lives. Thank you that our healthy, positive dreams come from you. What a difference you are making in Linda's and my life. We love you more, we love ourselves more and we love each other more. Thanks for sending us John and Jane. We ask you to give them wisdom and hope as they activate their plan. Thank you, Jesus, that your Holy Spirit is within us and you are closer to us than our problems. We love you, Amen.

Tears fill John's and Jane's eyes as they are hugged by this loving, caring twosome. Good-byes are exchanged and both couples go their separate ways.

If you have evaluated yourself proceed with your Five-Minute Plan, Worksheet *N*.

"One of the greatest reasons people cannot mobilize themselves is that they try to do great things. Most worthwhile achievements are a result of many little things done in a single direction."

Nido Qubein[2]

Step 5
One-Minute Appraisal

During the week John and Jane receive an invitation in the mail from a woman who belongs to Steve and Jenny's support group. They put the finishing touches on their Five-Minute Plan and accept her invitation to come for tea and dessert.

On Sunday, following the evening worship service at church, the Smiths arrive at her house. They ring the doorbell and find themselves facing a white-haired lady with an easy smile and eyes that sparkle. Her name is Jean and her gracious manner removes all their anxious feelings.

While they are being treated to a cup of tea and some homemade apple pie, the Smiths learn that Jean has become a widow. It has been a couple of years since her husband died and as they converse Jane notices a picture of Jean's husband and comments on what a fine-looking man he was.

Jean nods and smiles, "He certainly was handsome, but what I value most about our years together was the quality of our lives. I don't like to talk much about Dwight's heart attack or delve into great detail about how I felt, but needless to say there was quite an adjustment period.

"For quite a while I was starved for the affirmations my husband so freely gave. I guess I kept hoping others would pick up the slack. Quickly I had to face the reality that there was no choice. I could either feel sorry for myself or I could learn how to be an affirmer—both to myself and others. But I'm getting ahead of myself. Would you like another cup of tea?"

After succumbing to another cup of tea and one more sliver of pie, John and Jane both ask Jean to continue.

"Well," she says, "I don't know what I would've done if it hadn't been for the support group. They walked me through my time of intense grief and pain. I could keep you here all night telling you stories of the love they expressed to me."

Laughingly she adds, "Don't worry, I won't. I'm not forgetting why you came. One person in our group was particularly helpful to me at this stage. He's a financial consultant and I wanted him here this evening, but he's in Canada on business. His name is Gordon. He's the person who taught me how to appraise my progress. This is the next step."

Continuing on she says, "There were so many decisions to face after Dwight's death. I had the good sense to know that I couldn't attack all of them at once, so, with much prayer and counsel from my support group, I chose one pressing problem to work on. I made up my plan and broke it down into small steps. But I always focused on how far I had to go. All I could see was what I had *not* done.

"At a support group meeting one evening I expressed my frustration. Gordon listened patiently to me for some time and then took out a piece of blank paper. He told me I was defeating myself. Those were hard words to hear but he certainly got my attention.

"He then continued, 'You've only focused on a partial picture. In a way, Jean, you only see your problem and the distance from here to your goal. You haven't balanced that by appreciating yourself for what you've done right. You aren't giving yourself any credit.'

"Next he gave me a blank piece of paper and asked me to list the small steps necessary to achieve my goal. I was a little uncomfortable because this was happening in front of the entire support group. But you know what? *Everybody* had a blank piece of paper and was doing the same thing. They're quite a group!"

John breaks in, "They were all probably in the same boat. I know we would've been because I thought about how far we had to go when I wrote down our small steps the other evening." Jane nods in agreement.

Jean smiles, "Well, you know what I discovered? Four of the steps were completed! I hadn't even realized that.

"Then Gordon asked me a surprising question. 'What have you done to reward yourself?' Obviously I hadn't done a thing. I hadn't even acknowledged my progress.

Well, this delightful man turned to the rest of our support group and asked, 'Why don't we have dessert now instead of afterwards? Let's celebrate Jean's progress and yours.' We all laughed. Someone said that if they celebrated with food they'd have to change their goal from dieting. Anyway, dessert *was* served.

"But before we ate Gordon thanked the Lord for His goodness. Then he affirmed me to the Lord for my courage and thanked our precious Holy Spirit for giving me the power."

With eyes brimming with tears she says, "Nobody had prayed for me like that since Dwight's death. As you can imagine, I felt lifted and happy. I felt as if someone had given me permission to enjoy the process of achieving my goals.

"But enough of my experience," she states. "I have a blank piece of paper here. Why don't you list the small steps you've both chosen."

While John and Jane list their small steps, Jean makes some fresh tea and fills their china cups with the piping hot liquid. When she sees that they are finishing, she begins talking again.

"I realize you haven't had time to work on all your small steps, but what I'd like to do is help you set up a reward system. It's true that just accomplishing the step is its own reward, but somehow it's more fun to celebrate your progress. Anyway, if your focus is like mine was, you're oblivious to your own success."

Jane's eyes are sparkling now. "What we should do is catch ourselves doing something right and celebrate it," she says.

"That's right," replies Jean. "What are some meaningful rewards for you?"

"That's easy," laughs John. "I can think of a few like a game of tennis, a date night, a walk."

It's more rewarding to catch yourself doing something right than to be constantly expecting failure.

"Right," adds Jane. "Why don't we read a book together, go to a concert, or share a hot fudge sundae?"

Much laughter can be heard as the two set up their reward system. When they accomplish one step that leads them closer to their goal they will celebrate with a reward to reinforce their progress. Jane giggles, "This is going to be more fun than I ever imagined, isn't it?" John and Jean smile back at her.

"By the way," Jean continues, "that evening Gordon pulled a folded piece of paper out of his wallet. On it he'd written down some hints for handling everyday stress. He offered it to me. Of course, I made some copies and now I'd like you two to have one. He checks the list once or twice a day, just as a reminder, and that's what I've done with mine. It's entitled 'Gordon's Helpful Hints'—not too original but highly practical!" (See Worksheet *R*.)

"Thanks," respond the Smiths. "We're certainly willing to learn."

"I know you are," says Jean. "That makes it such a joy to share with you.

"Do you recall the prayer I said Gordon prayed at our dessert celebration?" John and Jane both nod that they do.

"Well," says Jean, "when I was in bed that evening, the words of that prayer came back to me. It was as if I'd been struck by lightning. Gordon had not only caught me doing things right, he'd affirmed who I was. He said I had a desire for excellence, courage and perseverance. I felt valued for who I was, not just for what I did. Not since Dwight's death had I felt that cherished.

"Suddenly I understood that it was a question of motivation. You often see affirmation used as a tool of manipulation, to get someone to do what you want. Gordon and my husband affirmed because they were both convinced, through their understanding of Scripture and psychology, that affirmation could help humans.

"As I lay in bed the Lord let me know that it was necessary for me to affirm my personal value, separate from my performance. He seemed to say, 'Jean, that's what I did on Calvary. I died for you while you were still a sinner.'

"That's what you're going to have to do. Affirm your performance! Catch yourself doing something right! You also need to affirm your character as valuable and precious whether you succeed or fail. We're used to facing criticism that attacks our *character,* not just our actions. When people only affirm our actions they make comments like, 'That was a great paper you wrote. That was a great dinner . . . etc.' They neglect to affirm our character.

"Well, the good news is, Jesus reverses this bad habit. He affirms our character *and* our actions. When He first met Simon, Jesus practiced character affirmation. He could have said, 'Simon, you're a good fisherman.' In this case Jesus would've focused only on Simon's actions. Instead, Jesus affirmed his character by giving Simon a new name, 'Peter,' which means rock.

"So, precious people," Jean smiles, "you need to become adept at step two of The One-Minute Appraisal. Affirm your value as separate from your performance. If you don't get good at it, you'll get discouraged when you face the last step in the Stress Reduction Plan."

If you have articulated your plan and have broken it down into small steps, proceed with your One-Minute Appraisal, Worksheet *S.*

Step 6
One-Minute Adjustment

Jean continues, "The final stage of our Stress Reduction Plan is the One-Minute Adjustment. As I mentioned, the necessary first step to adjusting your plan is to affirm your value as a person in spite of your performance."

Step 6
One-Minute Adjustment

"You mentioned that," responds John, "but I don't quite understand why."

"Then I'm glad you asked," smiles Jean. "It's because this type of affirmation gives us the motivation and the strength to keep going without feeling overwhelmed or like a failure.

"Mistakes don't mean I'm no good. For instance, if I start achieving some small steps leading towards my goal and then have to change some thinking or behavior that is interfering, it doesn't mean I'm a failure. It just means some changes need to be made."

"I understand now," responds John. "Our mistakes help us grow wiser."

"Honey, remember the statement we heard that television pastor give last Sunday?" asks Jane. "If you dare to try, you are a winner over the fear of failing."

"You two are special," adds Jean. "You're getting the idea. Instead of telling yourself, 'I'll never amount to anything, I blew it again!' say, 'Yes, I made a mistake, but I'm still a valuable and a greatly loved person. In fact, I'm also wiser.'

"All that is needed, then, is a slight mid-course correction. I have a sheet of paper here which you'll find helpful if you run into a roadblock. It's just a simple form that will help you deal with roadblocks." (See Worksheet *U*.)

"Thanks," respond the Smiths as they reach for the form.

"Remember," Jean says, "you may find it unnecessary to make an adjustment in your plans. But if you *do* find it necessary, make the adjustment, realizing that this has

Your God has declared you to be adequate. So risk, achieve and sometimes fail with a firm sense of your own adequacy.

nothing to do with your value as a person. Your God has declared you to be adequate so risk, achieve and sometimes fail with a firm sense of your own adequacy.

"When the wonderful day comes and you've achieved your goal, enjoy it and celebrate! But then what? This is the time for you to take out the Life-style Balance Assessment (Worksheet *V*) that I am giving you now. Together you can assess the balance, or lack of it, in your life. If you find an area of crucial need, that may be the next area you'll want to apply The Ten-Minute Stress Reduction Plan. It'll feel more natural the next time you go through it."

John and Jane accept Jean's checklist and thank her for the valuable information she's shared with them. They stay for another hour just enjoying this beautiful person who before tonight was a total stranger to them. Both feel as if they've known her all their lives. How much she has helped them! Sounds of happy conversation are heard as they clean up Jean's kitchen.

If you have appraised your progress proceed with your One-Minute Adjustment, Worksheet *T*.

The 10-Minute Stress Reduction Plan

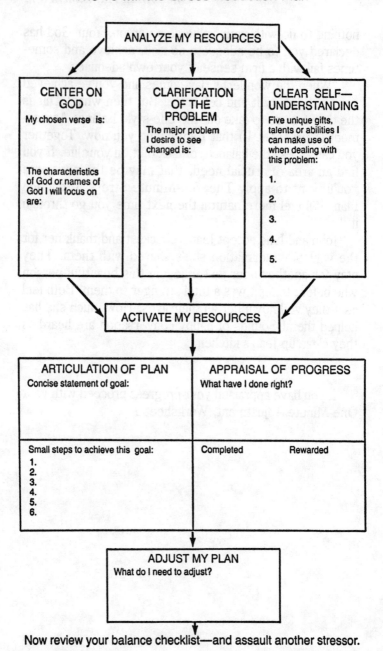

ANALYZE MY RESOURCES

CENTER ON GOD

My chosen verse is:

The characteristics of God or names of God I will focus on are:

CLARIFICATION OF THE PROBLEM

The major problem I desire to see changed is:

CLEAR SELF—UNDERSTANDING

Five unique gifts, talents or abilities I can make use of when dealing with this problem:

1.

2.

3.

4.

5.

ACTIVATE MY RESOURCES

ARTICULATION OF PLAN

Concise statement of goal:

APPRAISAL OF PROGRESS

What have I done right?

Small steps to achieve this goal:
1.
2.
3.
4.
5.
6.

Completed   Rewarded

ADJUST MY PLAN

What do I need to adjust?

Now review your balance checklist—and assault another stressor.

The Challenge

A month has gone by since the Smiths' conversation with Jean and they are making great strides towards achieving the goal they decided on. Each has experienced a renewed awareness of God's presence, a revitalized relationship with Him and a restored belief in their own value. They have stopped being victims of a stress-filled existence and have started to feel as if they are victors over one area of stress. They have a renewed hope that a balanced life-style is possible.

Suddenly one evening they receive a phone call. The cheerful voice on the other end of the line asks Jane, "What have you caught yourself doing right today?" Laughingly Jane calls to John, "It's Jean on the phone, honey, grab the extension."

For a few moments they converse. During that time Jean affirms both of them. Then she asks them if they would enjoy being a part of the support group that has been instrumentally used by the Lord to turn their lives around.

"By the way," Jean says, "we just heard about a couple whose marriage is near collapse because they're suffering from burnout. They've been asking Art questions. He wondered, as do we all, if you're ready to graduate from The 10-Minute Stress Reduction Plan."

She continues, "You two are such special people and I must confess I had no idea I'd be so blessed in the process. Thank you for that.

"The final step in The 10-Minute Stress Reduction Plan is to share your life with someone else who's struggling with high stress. Now it's your turn to pass it on."

Are *you* willing?

My personal value is separate from my performance. Because I know I am valuable I'm set free to achieve.

Your Personal 10-Minute
Stress Reduction Plan

One-Minute Centering

1. *Concentrate* on who God is.
   Refer to Worksheets *D*, "Names of Our Lord" and *E*,
   "Scripture Passages About God and His Care."

2. *Claim* God's personal interest in your life by
   personalizing and memorizing one of the Scriptures
   listed in Worksheet *E*. Use this as your stabilizing
   verse.

   My verse: _Come to me all you who labor_
   and are heavy laden and are burdened - and I
   will give you rest - I will ease & relieve
   & refresh your souls.

3. *Contact* His power through prayer.

Slow Me Down, Lord

Slow me down, Lord.
Ease the pounding of my heart by the quieting of my
    mind.
Steady my hurried pace with a vision of the eternal reach
    of time.
Give me, amid the confusion of the day, the calmness of
    the everlasting hills.
Break the tensions of my nerves and muscles with the
    soothing music of the singing streams that live in my
    memory.
Teach me the art of taking minute vacations—of slowing
    down to look at a flower, to chat with a friend, to pat a
    dog, to smile at a child, to read a few lines from a good
    book.
Slow me down, Lord, and inspire me to send my roots
    deep into the soil of life's enduring values, that I may
    grow toward my greater destiny.
Remind me each day that the race is not always to the
    swift; that there is more to life than increasing its
    speed.
Let me look upward to the towering oak and know that it
    grew great and strong because it grew slowly and
    well.[1]

St. Patrick's Breastplate

Christ be beside me, Christ be before me,
Christ be behind me, King of my heart.
Christ be within me, Christ be below me,
Christ be above me, Never to part.

Christ on my right hand, Christ on my left hand,
Christ all around me, Sealed in the strife.
Christ in my sleeping, Christ in my sitting,
Christ in my rising, Light of my life.

Christ be in all hearts Thinking about me,
Christ be on all tongues Telling of me,
Christ be the vision in eyes that see me,
In ears that hear me, Christ ever be. [2]

Sung to the tune of "Morning Is Broken"

Names of Our Lord

Jesus
Matthew 1:21
Prince of Peace
Isaiah 9:6
Mighty God
Isaiah 9:6
Wonderful Counselor
Isaiah 9:6
Holy One
Mark 1:24
Lamb of God
John 1:29
Prince of Life
Acts 3:15
Lord God Almighty
Revelation 15:3
Lion of the Tribe of Judah
Revelation 5:5
Root of David
Revelation 5:5
Word of Life
1 John 1:1
Author and Finisher of Our Faith
Hebrews 12:2
Advocate
1 John 2:1
The Way
John 14:6
Dayspring
Luke 1:78
Lord of All
Acts 10:36
I Am
John 8:58
Son of God
John 1:34

Messiah
John 1:41
The Truth
John 14:6
Saviour
2 Peter 2:20
Chief Cornerstone
Ephesians 2:20
King of Kings
Revelation 19:16
Righteous Judge
2 Timothy 4:8
Light of the World
John 8:12
Head of the Church
Ephesians 1:22
Morning Star
Revelation 22:16
Sun of Righteousness
Malachi 4:2
Lord Jesus Christ
Acts 15:11

Chief Shepherd
1 Peter 5:4
Resurrection and Life
John 11:25
Horn of Salvation
Luke 1:69
Governor
Matthew 2:6
Alpha and Omega
Revelation 1:8
Shepherd and Bishop of Souls
1 Peter 2:25

Scripture Passages About God and His Care

From *The Amplified Bible:*

"I am the Vine, you are the branches. Whoever lives in Me and I in him bears much (abundant) fruit. However, apart from Me—cut off from vital union with Me—you can do nothing" (John 15:5).

"Teaching them to observe everything that I have commanded you, and lo, I am with you all the days—perpetually, uniformly and on every occasion—to the [very] close and consummation of the age. Amen—so let it be" (Matt. 28:20).

"That they may become progressively more intimately acquainted with, and may know more definitely and accurately and thoroughly, that mystic secret of God [which is] Christ, the Anointed One. In Him all the treasures of [divine] wisdom, [of comprehensive insight into the ways and purposes of God], and [all the riches of spiritual] knowledge and enlightenment are stored up and lie hidden" (Col. 2:2-3).

"But He said to me, My grace—My favor and loving-kindness and mercy—are enough for you, [that is, sufficient against any danger and to enable you to bear the trouble manfully]; for My strength and power are made perfect—fulfilled and completed and show themselves most effective—in [your] weakness" (2 Cor. 12:9).

"Do not fret or have any anxiety about anything, but in every circumstance and in everything by prayer and petition [definite requests] with thanksgiving continue to make your wants known to God. And God's peace [be yours, that tranquil state of a soul assured of its salvation through Christ, and so fearing nothing from God and content with its earthly lot of whatever sort that is, that peace] which transcends all understanding, shall garrison and mount guard over your hearts and minds in Christ Jesus" (Phil. 4:6-7).

"Casting the whole of your care—all your anxieties, all your worries, all your concerns, once and for all—on Him; for He cares for you affectionately, and cares about you watchfully" (1 Pet. 5:7).

"Little children, you are of God—you belong to Him—and have [already] defeated and overcome them [the agents of antichrist], because He Who lives in you is greater (mightier) than he who is in the world" (1 John 4:4).

"For we are God's [own] handiwork (His workmanship), recreated in Christ Jesus, [born anew] that we may do those good works which God predestined (planned beforehand) for us, (taking paths which He prepared ahead of time) that we should walk in them—living the good life which He prearranged and made ready for us to live" (Eph. 2:10).

"The steps of a [good] man are directed and established of the Lord, when He delights in his way [and He busies Himself with his every step]. Though he fall, he shall not be utterly cast down, for the Lord grasps his hand in support and upholds him" (Ps. 37:23-24).

"Fear not; [there is nothing to fear] for I am with you; do not look around you in terror and be dismayed, for I am your God. I will strengthen and harden you [to difficulties];

yes, I will help you; yes, I will hold you up and retain you with My victorious right hand of rightness and justice. For I, the Lord your God, hold your right hand; I, Who say to you, Fear not, I will help you!" (Isa. 41:10,13).

"For whatever is born of God is victorious over the world; and this is the victory that conquers the world, even our faith. Who is it that is victorious over (that conquers) the world but he who believes that Jesus is the Son of God— who adheres to, trusts in and relies [on that fact]?" (1 John 5:4-5).

"Although my father and my mother have forsaken me, yet the Lord will take me up [adopt me as His child]" (Ps. 27:10).

"We are hedged in [pressed] on every side—troubled and oppressed in every way; but not cramped or crushed; we suffer embarrassments and are perplexed and unable to find a way out, but not driven to despair; We are [persecuted and hard driven,] pursued, but not deserted—to stand alone; we are struck down to the ground, but never struck out and destroyed" (2 Cor. 4:8-9).

"Let us then fearlessly and confidently and boldly draw near to the throne of grace—the throne of God's unmerited favor [to us sinners]; that we may receive mercy [for our failures] and find grace to help in good time for every need—appropriate help and well-timed help, coming just when we need it" (Heb. 4:16).

"Come to Me, all you who labor and are heavy-laden and over-burdened, and I will cause you to rest—I will ease and relieve and refresh your souls" (Matt. 11:28).

"And my God will liberally supply (fill to the full) your

every need according to His riches in glory in Christ Jesus" (Phil. 4:19).

"I will say of the Lord, He is my refuge and my fortress, my God, on Him I lean and rely, and in Him I (confidently) trust! For [then] He will deliver you from the snare of the fowler and from the deadly pestilence. [Then] He will cover you with His pinions, and under His wings shall you trust and find refuge; His truth and His faithfulness are a shield and a buckler" (Ps. 91:2-4).

"Lean on, trust and be confident in the Lord with all your heart and mind, and do not rely on your own insight or understanding. In all your ways know, recognize and acknowledge Him, and He will direct and make straight and plain your paths" (Prov. 3:5-6).

"The Lord is my light and my salvation; whom shall I fear or dread? The Lord is the refuge and stronghold of my life; of whom shall I be afraid?" (Ps. 27:1).

"Have the roots [of your being] firmly and deeply planted [in Him]—fixed and founded in Him—being continually built up in Him, becoming increasingly more confirmed and established in the faith, just as you were taught, and abounding and overflowing in it with thanksgiving" (Col. 2:7).

"And this is the confidence—the assurance, the [privilege of] boldness—which we have in Him; [we are sure] that if we ask anything (make any request) according to His will (in agreement with His own plan) He listens to and hears us. And if (since) we (positively) know that He listens to us in whatever we ask, we also know [with settled and absolute knowledge] that we have [granted us as our present possessions] the requests made of Him" (1 John 5:14-15).

"If you live in Me—abide vitally united to Me—and My words remain in you and continue to live in your hearts, ask whatever you will and it shall be done for you" (John 15:7).

From the *King James Version*:

"Peace I leave with you, my peace I give unto you: not as the world giveth, give I unto you. Let not your heart be troubled, neither let it be afraid" (John 14:27).

"Forgetting those things which are behind, and reaching forth unto those things which are before, I press toward the mark for the prize of the high calling of God in Christ Jesus" (Phil. 3:13-14).

"Thou wilt keep him in perfect peace, whose mind is stayed on thee: because he trusteth in thee" (Isa. 26:3).

"Come unto me, all *ye* that labour and are heavy laden, and I will give you rest" (Matt. 11:28).

"To be spiritually minded *is* life and peace" (Rom. 8:6).

"That we may lead a quiet and peaceable life in all godliness and honesty. For this *is* good and acceptable in the sight of God our Saviour" (1 Tim. 2:2-3).

"I will both lay me down in peace, and sleep: for thou, Lord, only makest me dwell in safety" (Ps. 4:8).

"I will lift up mine eyes unto the hills, from whence cometh my help. My help cometh from the Lord, which made my help. My help cometh from the Lord, which made heaven and earth" (Ps. 121:1-2).

"Surely goodness and mercy shall follow me all the days of my life: and I will dwell in the house of the Lord for ever" (Ps. 23:6).

The Lord *is* my helper, and I will not fear what man shall do unto me" (Heb. 13:6).

One-Minute Clarification

1. *Check* the areas causing you the most stress by referring to Worksheet *F*, "Where Stress Comes From."

2. *Challenge* your general expectations. Are you making unrealistic demands on yourself?

3. *Concentrate* on a clear definition of the problem by writing down a concise sentence stating the major problem you are confronting at this time:

_____

_____

_____

_____

Where Stress Comes From

Which of these areas is causing you the greatest stress?

_____ Chemicals
_____ Children
_____ Communication
_____ Commuting
_____ Major decision-making
_____ Emotions
_____ Finances
_____ Health (sleeping, eating, disease, sickness, etc.)
_____ Investments
_____ Life changes (empty nest, adolescence, etc.)
_____ Life traumas (divorce, death, etc.)
_____ Marital problems
_____ Physical challenges
_____ Phobias
_____ Recreation
_____ Relationships
_____ Low self-esteem
_____ Sexual problems
_____ Spiritual needs
_____ Time
_____ Work
_____ Vacation
_____ Other _____

Expectations Checklist

Please check those statements describing the
expectations you hold for yourself.

_____ 1. I should excel at everything.

_____ 2. I should not be tired.

_____ 3. I should not raise my voice when angry.

___✓__ 4. I should always be available to my friends.

___✓__ 5. I should always be positive.

___✓__ 6. I should always be enthusiastic.

___✓__ 7. I should be a model of success for my peers.

___✓__ 8. I should provide a good standard of living for
my family.

_____ 9. I should be more productive.

_____ 10. I should exercise daily.

___✓__ 11. I should read my Bible and pray daily.

_____ 12. I should be creative.

_____ 13. I should be friendly.

_____ 14. I should own a nice home.

_____ 15. I should be outgoing.

_____ 16. I should be more businesslike.

_____ 17. I should not let problems get me down.

_____ 18. I should be more organized.

_____ 19. I should be able to handle this problem on my own.

_____ 20. I should prove myself in all situations.

_____ 21. I should have a dream.

_____ 22. I should not be overweight.

_____ 23. I should not make mistakes.

_____ 24. I should never give up.

_____ 25. I should constantly push myself to the limit.

_____ 26. I should always finish what I'm doing before moving on to the next project.

_____ 27. I should have new interests.

_____ 28. I should not expect rewards for my ministry.

_____ 29. I should be more hospitable.

_____ 30. I should attend all my children's activities.

_____ 31. I should be a friend as well as a parent to my children.

_____ 32. I should spend more time with my spouse and/or children.

_____ 33. I shouldn't have to ask for more pay. My value should be obvious.

_____ 34. I should always look attractive.

_____ 35. I should reach all my goals.

_____ 36. I should never say no.

_____ 37. I should always feel sexy.

_____ 38. I should always feel accepted.

_____ 39. I should always feel competent.

_____ 40. I should use every moment productively.

If you have checked 20 or more sentences you are setting yourself up for disillusionment. *You* are the major cause of your own stress.

Reexamine the expectations you've placed on yourself. Are you trying to prove your adequacy to God and to others?

Release the internal pressure you are applying to yourself by eliminating the "shoulds" in your life.

Two Important Questions

1. What has the potential to make me extremely angry about this stressful situation?

2. What am I worrying about? Complete this sentence as it relates to your particular stress.

One-Minute Self-Evaluation

1. *Emphasize* God's positive view of you. See Worksheet
   K.

2. *Evaluate* your beliefs by referring to Worksheet *L.*
   Are they healthy or unhealthy?

3. *Examine* your traits, talents, gifts, experiences,
   contacts, strengths and weaknesses. Thank the Lord
   who is completing and has completed these aspects in
   you.

How God Sees Me!

We were created in God's image.	Genesis 1:26-27
God formed our inward parts.	Psalm 139:13
God created an inherent goodness into Adam and Eve.	Genesis 1:31
We are the image and glory of God.	1 Corinthians 11:7
We are the culmination of God's creativity.	Genesis 1:26
We are given dominion over the earth.	Genesis 1:28
God created us a little lower than the angels.	Psalm 8:5
Angels care for us.	Hebrews 1:14; Matthew 18:10
Our purchase price is beyond calculation.	1 Peter 1:18-19
God values each person highly.	Luke 7:28
God loves us even as sinners.	Romans 5:8
We are justified in Christ.	Romans 3:26
There is no condemnation to those in Christ.	Romans 8:1
We are temples of God.	1 Corinthians 3:16
We are new creatures in Christ.	2 Corinthians 5:17-21
We are holy and blameless	Ephesians 1:4; Colossians 1:22
We are a chosen people.	1 Peter 2:9
God causes our growth.	1 Corinthians 3:7; Philippians 2:13
We can do all things through Christ.	Philippians 4:13
Our steps are directed by the Lord.	Psalm 37:23-24
Apart from God we can do nothing.	John 15:5
We are empowered through our union with God.	Ephesians 6:10
God will withhold nothing from those who walk uprightly.	Psalm 84:11
God greatly loves and prizes us.	John 3:16
God gives us His peace.	John 14:27
God sets us free.	John 8:36

Worksheet K

Evaluate Your Beliefs

Positive, Healthy and Balanced Beliefs

- It is NOT necessary to be liked by everyone.

- I do NOT have to earn anyone's approval or acceptance to be a person of worth.

- I am a child of God. I'm deeply loved by Him, and I have been forgiven by Him; therefore I am acceptable. I accept myself.

- My needs and wants are as important as other people's.

- Rejection is NOT terrible. It may be a bit unpleasant, but it is not terrible.

- Not being approved of or accepted is NOT terrible. It may not be desirable, but it is not terrible.

- If somebody doesn't like me, I can live with it. I don't have to work feverishly to get him/her to like me.

- I can conquer my bad feelings by distinguishing the truth from misbelief.

- It is a misbelief that I must please other people and be approved by them.

- Jesus died on a cross for me so that I can be free from the misbelief that other people decide my value. [3]

My Personal Assets

1. What qualities best describe me? Check between three and five qualities.

___ achiever	___ intelligent
___ active	___ interdependent
___ affirmer	___ investigator
___ appraiser	___ motivator
___ artistic, creative	___ objective thinker
___ attractive	___ passive
___ conventional	___ perfectionist
___ cooperative	___ persuader
___ counselor	___ practical
___ dependent	___ promoter
___ follower	___ result-oriented
___ independent	___ sociable
___ instructor	___ structured

2. My data bank

   a. What past training or education have I had which may bear on this problem?

   b. Who from my past can help me with my problem?

c. What talents have I developed which can be of use to me now?

d. What resource materials, including tapes, books, films, TV, articles, etc., can be a part of the solution?

e. What previous experience relates to this problem?

f. My five greatest strengths are:

g. My three greatest weaknesses are:

h. What personal qualities can I most effectively use to help solve this problem?

Five-Minute Plan

1. *Propose* possible solutions to the problem.

2. *Pinpoint* the best solution and write it down on Worksheet *P*.

3. *Program* your solution by breaking it down into measurable, time-related steps.

4. *Picture* yourself achieving your goal and enjoying the benefits of your accomplishment.

Relaxation Response

1. Sit quietly in a comfortable position with your feet flat on the floor and hands separated but resting on your lap.

2. Close your eyes.

3. Use the following method to progressively and deeply relax all your muscles, beginning at your feet. Work your way up your body to your face. Keep muscles relaxed as you proceed.

    a. Tense each muscle group, e.g., feet, calves, etc.

    b. Hold tension approximately five seconds.

    c. Release the tension slowly, at the same time thinking, "Relax and let go."

    d. Take a deep breath.

    e. As you breathe slowly out, think, "Relax and let go."

4. This relaxation process will take you between 15 and 20 minutes to complete.

5. When you finish sit quietly for several minutes, at first with your eyes closed and later with them open. Do not stand up for a few minutes.

6. If you are not successful in achieving relaxation the first few times do not worry—most individuals do not. Permit relaxation to occur at its own pace. When distracting thoughts come, try to ignore them by refocusing on the relaxation procedure. With a little practice you will be successful.[4]

Worksheet O

Problems and Solutions Go Hand 'n Hand

The problem I want to work on: _____

_____

_____

_____

_____

_____

_____

Possible solutions to this problem: _____

_____

_____

_____

_____

_____

_____

_____

Programming My Solution into Measurable, Time-Related Steps

My chosen solution is: _____

_____

_____

9.

8.

7.

6.

5.

4.

3.

2.

1.

How will I feel when I achieve my goal?

_____

_____

_____

Gordon's Helpful Hints

1. Spread unpleasant tasks between those tasks you enjoy.

2. Assess your most productive time. Block it off for creative work.

3. Make a quick telephone call to a "nourisher"—someone who affirms you in the midst of a busy day.

4. Develop a mentor you can go to for counsel.

5. Take a "one-minute vacation"—by praying for someone, hugging someone, going outside to stretch or yell or thanking someone who works at your office. Read *When I Relax I Feel Guilty* by Tim Hansel.

6. Make a "Not to Do" list that includes minor time wasters like extended telephone calls, lengthy meetings of minor importance, shuffling of mail, extended lunch hours.

7. Make a "To Do" list.

8. Eliminate and concentrate. (Read *Disciplines of a Beautiful Woman* by Anne Ortlund or *How to Get Control of Your Time and Your Life* by A. Lakein). Now complete a project.

9. Delegate tasks where possible.

10. Improve your skills by reading a book, taking a class or attending a seminar.

11. Take time to laugh. Remember, "A merry heart doeth good like a medicine" (Prov. 17:22, *KJV*).

12. Separate from your work at the end of the day by casting your care upon God during the evening.

*13. Exercise regularly—at least four times per week.
*14. Average between 7½ and 8 hours of sleep every night.
*15. Be aware of your nutrition by:
   A. Restricting sugars;
   B. Increasing the fruits, nuts, grain and vegetables you eat;
   C. Eating lots of fish and poultry;
   D. Skipping between-meal snacks—except nutritional nibbling which includes nuts and fruits;
   E. Eliminating cigarette smoking;
   F. Maintaining your optimum weight;
   G. Making breakfast your biggest meal;
   H. Drinking alcohol in moderation.

* These nutrition tips will add 11 years to your life according to a 1983 study conducted by the California Department of Public Health.

One-Minute Appraisal

1. *Appraise* your plan by filling out the chart below.
   a. List the small steps you decided to take on Worksheet P.
   b. What progress have you made?
   c. Decide on some meaningful rewards—you deserve it!
2. *Affirm* your value as separate from your performance.

Small Steps	Positive Progress	Rewards
A.	A.	A.
B.	B.	B.
C.	C.	C.
D.	D.	D.
E.	E.	E.
F.	F.	F.
G.	G.	G.
H.	H.	H.
I.	I.	I.

Worksheet S

One-Minute Adjustment

1. *Acknowledge* any thinking or behavior that may be interfering with your efforts to reach your goals.

2. *Adjust* to overcome your roadblocks by using Worksheet *U*.

3. *Assess* the balances in your life-style by completing Worksheet *V*.

Now *assault* another of life's stressors!

One-Minute Adjustment

Roadblocks	Small Steps to Overcome Roadblocks

"If you dare to try you are a winner
over the fear of failing."

Robert H. Schuller[5]

Worksheet U

Life-Style Balance Assessment

Goal: A balanced life-style.

Life-Style

	Out of Control	Moving Away from Balance	Moving Towards Balance	Balanced
1. I take time for myself.				
2. I allow for periods of relaxation.				
3. When I am tired I rest.				
4. I develop new interests and hobbies.				
5. I take time for my appearance.				
6. I take time for meditation, devotions and prayer.				
7. I maintain healthy eating habits.				
8. I maintain a healthy weight.				
9. I maintain and develop my sense of humor.				
10. I take time to plan.				
11. I take time for a date night.				

Life-Style	Out of Control	Moving Away from Balance	Moving Towards Balance	Balanced
12. I am self-aware.				
13. I am physically healthy.				
14. I take time to work on my marriage.				
15. I spend quality time with my children.				
16. I maintain old relationships.				
17. I take time to develop new relationships.				
18. I have a support group.				
19. I deal with interpersonal conflict.				
20. Forgiving is a high priority.				
21. I make my deadlines.				
22. I take time for my occupation.				
23. Facing my anger is a high priority.				
24. I need others' approval.				

Worksheet V (2)

Life-Style	Out of Control	Moving Away from Balance	Moving Towards Balance	Balanced
25. I live in the present rather than in the past.				
26. I acknowledge my mistakes and see them as necessary for my growth.				
27. I have a healthy sex life.				
28. I take one day off a week.				
29. I feel as if I am in control of my time.				
30. I feel as if I'm adapting to the changes brought on by my age.				
31. I feel like I'm adapting to those unexpected life crises				
32. I can assertively express my needs and beliefs.				
33. I am learning to face my fears.				
34. I feel spiritually nourished by my belief in God.				
35. I feel I am a person of worth and value.				
36. I am in control of my finances.				

Worksheet V (3)

Notes

Introduction

1. We're referring to the June, 1983 issue of *Time* Magazine.

Step 2: One-Minute Clarification

1. Lloyd John Ogilvie, *Making Stress Work for You* (Waco, TX: Word Books, 1984), p. 43.

Step 3: One-Minute Self-Evaluation

1. H. Norman Wright, *Improving Your Self-Image* (Eugene, OR: Harvest House, 1983), p. 32.

Step 4: Five-Minute Plan

1. Robert A. Schuller, source unknown.
2. Nido Qubein, *Get the Best from Yourself* (Englewood Cliffs, NJ: Prenctice Hall, Inc., 1983), p. 100.

Your Personal 10-Minute Stress Reduction Plan

1. "Slow Me Down, Lord," by Orin L. Crain, in *When I Relax I Feel Guilty* by Tim Hansel (Elgin, IL: David C. Cook Publishing Co., 1979).

2. English hymn, source unknown.

3. H. Norman Wright, *Improving Your Self-Image* (Eugene, OR: Harvest House Publishers, 1983), pp. 91-92.

4. This is adapted from *The Relaxation Response* by M. Benson and *Stress Management* by E. Charlesworth and R. Nathan.

5. Quote is from the 1984 Possibility Thinker's Calendar, published by the Robert Schuller Ministries.

Bibliography for Further Reading

A Research Overview

Dr. Hans Selye is often considered the "father of stress research." He did the pioneer work and was the first to connect physiological response with stress. He has published numerous books and articles. H. J. Freudenberger coined the term "burnout" in the early 1970s. He is a psychoanalyst who feels that burnout is caused by personality factors and internal drives. Opposing this explanation is C. Maslach, a social psychologist who claims burnout can best be understood and treated by addressing environmental factors. These two leading authorities form the basis for subsequent researchers who tend to align with either one side or the other in the continuing debate regarding burnout.

More recently a third, more holistic perspective has been proposed by David Congo, in his doctoral dissertation, and by L. J. Heifetz and H. A. Bersani. They all believe both external and internal factors, in combination, lead to burnout. There is much confusion and controversy about burnout and its similarities to and differences from stress. For further discussion of this issue read *Understanding Burnout* by A. Hart.

Research into burnout, as it affects many individual professions, is burgeoning. Professions such as teachers, nurses, social workers, policemen, probation officers, ministers, psychiatrists, psychologists, doctors, attorneys, child-care workers, agency administrators, business executives and parents have all been studied. If you have an interest in a particular profession's burnout, a list of recent research can be obtained by consulting C. Maslach at the University of California at Berkeley. Research into ministerial burnout, in particular, is continuing at Rosemead School of Psychology, Biola University, La Mirada, California.

Measurement of burnout continues to be a problem, but the most widely used instrument at this time is the Maslach Burnout Inventory (MBI) which can be obtained by writing to C. Maslach at the University of California at Berkeley. Another burnout test that can be used to make a simple burnout evaluation was developed by Lyle Miller and Alma Smith of Boston University Medical Center. It consists of 20 questions and was published in *Time* magazine on June 6, 1983.

The books listed in this bibliography will provide you with an excellent resource base. The first section of the bibliography lists general books on stress and burnout. Following this general section are books related to the major steps of *The 10-Minute Stress Reduction Plan*.

General Books on Stress and Burnout

Ahlem, Lloyd H. *Living with Stress*. Ventura, CA: Regal Books, 1978.

Albrecht, K. *Stress and the Manager.* Englewood Cliffs, NJ: Prentice-Hall, Inc., 1979.

Bratcher, E. *The Walk-on-Water Syndrome.* Waco, TX: Word Books, 1984.

Charlesworth, E., and Nathan, G. *Stress Management: A Comprehensive Guide to Wellness.* New York: Atheneum, 1984.

Collins, Gary. *You Can Profit from Stress.* Santa Ana, CA: Vision House, 1977.

Congo, David. The Role of Interpersonal Relationship Style, Life Change Events and Personal Data Variables in Ministerial Burnout. Unpublished Doctoral dissertation, Biola University, 1983.

Congo, David. "What Causes Burnout?" *Theology News and Notes,* vol. 31, 1984.

Freudenberger, H. J. *The Staff Burn-Out Syndrome.* Washington, D.C.: Drug Abuse Council, 1975a.

Freudenberger, H. J. "The Staff Burn-Out Syndrome in Alternative Institutions." *Psychotherapy: Theory, Research and Practice,* Vol. 12(1), Spring, 1975b.

Freudenberger, H. J. *Burnout: The High Cost of High Achievement.* Garden City, NJ: Doubleday and Co., 1980.

Hart, A. "Understanding Burnout." *Fuller's Theology News and Notes,* Vol. 31, 1984.

Heifetz, L., and Bersani, H. "Disrupting the Cybernetics of Personal Growth: Toward a Unified Theory of Burnout in the Human Services." *Stress and Burnout in the Human Service Professions.* New York: Pergamon Press, 1983.

Levinson, H. *Executive Stress.* New York: Mentor, 1975.

Maslach, C. *Burnout—The Cost of Caring.* Englewood Cliffs, NJ: Prentice-Hall, 1982.

Ogilvie, Lloyd John. *Making Stress Work for You.* Waco, TX: Word Books, 1984.

Procaccini, J., and Kiefaber, M. *Parent-Burnout.* New York: Doubleday & Co., 1983.

Rassieur, C. *Stress Management for Ministers.* Philadelphia, PA: Westminster, 1982.

Selye, Hans. *Stress Without Distress.* New York: Lippincott, 1980.

Witkin-Lanoil, G. *The Female Stress Syndrome.* New York: Newmarket Press, 1984.

Wright, Norman. *Crisis Counseling: Helping People in Crisis.* San Bernardino, CA: Here's Life, 1985.

Books Related to Major Points of Book

1. Centering on God

Foster, Richard. *Celebration of Discipline.* San Francisco CA: Harper & Row, 1978.

Lawrence. *Practicing the Presence of God.* Grand Rapids: Baker Book House, 1975.

Ortlund, Raymond. *Lord, Make My Life a Miracle.* Ventura, CA: Regal, 1974.

Peale, Norman Vincent. *Positive Imaging.* New York: Fawcett Crest, 1982.

2. Clarification of the Problem

Blanchard, Kenneth, and Johnson, Spencer. *One-Minute Manager.* New York: Berkeley Books, 1982.

Holmes, T., and Rahe, R. "Social Readjustment Rating Scale." *Journal of Psychosomatic Research,* Vol. 11, 1967.

Peters, T., and Waterman, R. *In Search of Excellence.* New York: Warner Books, 1982.

Wright, Norman. *Improving Your Self-Image.* Eugene, OR: Harvest House, 1983.

3. Self-Evaluation

Congo, Janet. *Finding Inner Security: A Woman's Quest for Interdependence.* Ventura, CA: Regal Books, 1985.

Gendlin, E. *Focusing.* New York: Everett House Publishers, 1978.

Geier, J. *Personal Profile System.* A self-scoring test which promotes self-understanding. (Order from Family

Counseling, 1913 E. 17th St., #118, Santa Ana, CA, 92701.)

Keirsey, D., and Bates, M. *Please Understand Me.* Del Mar, CA: Prometheus Nemesis Books, 1978.

McDowell, J. *His Image, My Image.* San Bernardino, CA: Here's Life Publishers, 1984.

Missildine, W. *Your Inner Child of the Past.* New York: Simon and Schuster, 1963.

Myers, I. *Gifts Differing.* Palo Alto, CA: Consulting Psychologists Press, Inc., 1980.

Stoop, D. *Self-Talk.* Old Tappan, NJ: Fleming H. Revell, 1982.

Taylor, R., and Johnson R. *Taylor-Johnson Temperament Analysis Test.* (Order from Psychological Publications, 5300 Hollywood Blvd., Los Angeles, CA 90027.)

Waitley, Denis. *Seeds of Greatness.* Old Tappan, NJ: Fleming H. Revell, 1983.

Wagner, M. *The Sensation of Being Somebody.* Grand Rapids: Zondervan Publishing, 1975.

4. Articulation of the Plan

Benson, H. *The Relaxation Response.* New York: Avon, 1975.

Blanchard, Kenneth, and Johnson, Spencer. *The One-Minute Manager.* New York: Berkeley Books, 1982.

Dayton, Edward, and Engstrom, Ted. *Strategy for Living.* Ventura, CA: Regal Books, 1976.

Jacobson, E. *Progressive Relaxation.* Chicago: University of Chicago, 1974.

Lakein, A. *How to Get Control of Your Time and Your Life.* New York: Peter H. Wyden, Inc., 1973.

Ortlund, Anne. *The Disciplines of the Beautiful Woman.* Waco, TX: Word Books, 1977.

Waitley, Denis. *The Double Win.* Old Tappan, NJ: Fleming H. Revell, 1985.

Waitley, Denis. *Seeds of Greatness.* Old Tappan, NJ: Fleming H. Revell, 1983.

Winston, S. *Getting Organized.* New York: Warner, 1978.

5. Appraisal of Your Progress

Blanchard, Kenneth, and Johnson, Spencer. *The One-Minute Manager.* New York: Berkeley Books, 1982.

Lutzer, E. *Failures. 1ne Backdoor to Success.* Chicago: Moody Press, 1975.

Qubein, Nido. *Get the Best from Yourself.* Englewood Cliffs, NJ: Prentice-Hall, Inc., 1983.

6. Adjustment of the Plan

Hansel, Tim. *When I Relax I Feel Guilty.* Elgin, IL: David C. Cook Publishing Co., 1979.

Levinson, D. *The Seasons of a Man's Life.* New York: Knopf, 1978.

Sheehy, Gail. *Passages: Predictable Crisis of Adult Life.* New York: Bantam Books, 1977.